بِسْمِ اللّٰهِ الرَّحْمٰنِ الرَّحِيمِ

BismiLlahi r-Rahmani r-Rahim

"In the name of Allah the most Kind, the most Caring

If you ask blessings on the Prophet 10 times you are rewarded 100 times.

If you ask blessings on the Prophet 100 times you are rewarded 1,000 times.

If you ask blessings on the Prophet 1,000 times you will receive a light on the Day of Resurrection, cross the bridge untouched by fire, and find a palace prepared for you in the Garden."

(Hadith cited by Imam al-Jazuli in his forward to Dalailu l-Khayrat).

Other Titles By This Author:

My Little Lore of Light
The Light of Muhammad
Links of Light: The Golden Chain
The Story of Moses
Who Are You? A Book of Very Serious Questions
The Animals of Paradise
The Animals of Paradise: Coloring Book

Printed in the United States of America ISBN 978-0-9913003-3-4

Little Bird Books littlebirdbooksink@gmail.com

Every Day
A Thousand
Times

By
Karima Sperling

Dedication

We cannot think about Dalailu l-Khayrat without also thinking about Hajja Amina Adil. The two are connected inseparably for those of us who knew her. After taking care of her large family and serving her many guests with care and patience, she never left a day empty of the blessings of reading Dalailu l-Khayrat. And she impressed deeply on the rest of us its value and importance.

"And Allah, Jalla Jallalahu, says: O My angels, this is one of My servants, who has asked for abundant blessings upon My beloved Muhammad, so by My Power, My Glory, My Generosity, My Splendor, My Sublimity, I grant him for every letter of the words asking for blessings a castle in the garden.

I will make him come to Me on the Day of Resurrection beneath the flag of praise, and the light of his face will be like the full moon and he will be hand in hand with My beloved Muhammad."

(Dalailu l-Khayrat by Imam al-Jazuli translated by Andrey Rosowsky. Great Books of the Islamic World.)

And to Haniya, Humayra, Layka, Ishaq, Jacob, Hamza, Ghalib, Khalil, Noura, Karima, Tarik, and Hala who love their Prophet (sas).

Thanks

Thank you to Aminah Alptekin for her enthusiasm for the project and her computer skills and design sense; to Munir Sperling, Alia Nazeer, and Fatima Sperling for multiple readings and advice; to Adam Sperling and Saad Al Kenany for scientific correction and direction; and to Hajja Rukiye Alptekin for advice and inspiration.

Introduction

Verily Allah and His Angels bless the Prophet. O you who believe, ask blessings on him and greet him with a greeting of peace. (33:56)

The verses of this small book are taken loosely from the Friday portion of Dalailu l-Khayrat by Imam al-Jazuli. It is a recommended practice to read a portion of that book every day. In a similar fashion it would be nice to read this book with children every night as the last book before bedtime, or to read it on days like Friday and Monday when it is said that praises on the Prophet are most desirable, or on special occasions like Eid and Mawlid. It will hopefully provide a calm and quiet moment for parent and child to remember their Prophet together and think about the wonder of the world that was created because of him and to think about the Lord Allah, whose power and majesty are reflected, at least partially, in the awesomeness of His creation.

The Prophet was neither short nor tall. His hair was dark, neither curly nor completely straight. His face was full and bright like the moon. His eyes were dark and his lashes long and black. His manner was gentle and easy going. He did not look for faults either in people or in what they did. He smiled often but laughed rarely.

He was open and friendly to all. He sat among people as one of them. His voice was soft and kind. Often he kept silent but when he spoke his words were clear and to the point. He listened when others spoke and he turned toward them to give his full attention. He loved to help people.

Those who saw him from far away thought he was beautiful. Those who saw him close up, loved him. Everyone agrees that they never saw, before or after, anyone like him.

"We have not sent you (Muhammad) except as a mercy for the worlds."
(21:107)

Bismi Llahi r-Rahmani r-Rahim

In the name of Allah, the most Kind, the most Caring.

بسم الله الرحمن الرحيم

O Allah, 124,000 of Your prophets came.
And each one prayed to You by a different name,
Although You are One and remain always the same.
Now we ask You by those most holy of names
To bless our Prophet Muhammad, sall Allahu alayhi wa s-sallam.

By the names Adam prayed, as-salamu alayh,
By the names Nuh prayed, as-salamu alayh,
By the names Hud prayed, as-salamu alayh,
By the names Ibrahim prayed, as-salamu alayh,
By the names Salih prayed, as-salamu alayh,
By the names Ayyub prayed, as-salamu alayh,
By the names Yunus prayed, as-salamu alayh,
By the names Ya'qub prayed, as-salamu alayh,
By the names Yusuf prayed, as-salamu alayh,
By the names Musa prayed, as-salamu alayh,
By the names Harun prayed, as-salamu alayh,
By the names Shu'ayb prayed, as-salamu alayh,
By the names Ismail prayed, as-salamu alayh,
By the names Da'ud prayed, as-salamu alayh,
By the names Sulayman prayed, as-salamu alayh,
By the names Zakariyya prayed, as-salamu alayh,
By the names Yahya prayed, as-salamu alayh,
By the names Armiya prayed, as-salamu alayh,
By the names Yusha' prayed, as-salamu alayh,
By the names 'Isa prayed, as-salamu alayh,
By the names Muhammad prayed,
    sall Allahu alayhi wa s-sallam.

We ask You to bless all the prophets, known and unknown.

Their faces were different but their light was one -

Bless the light of Muhammad wherever it shone.

O Allah, we ask You to bless our Prophet Muhammad
as much as the day takes turns with the night,
as much as the darkness hides and the dawn brings to light,
from the day You created the world until the day it ends,
every day a thousand times.

O Allah, we ask You to bless our Prophet Muhammad
as much as the circling of planets and the pulsing of stars,
as much as the glorifying of angels and the beating of hearts,
from the day You created the world until the day it ends,
every day a thousand times.

O Allah, we ask You to bless our Prophet Muhammad
as much as the rocks and gravel and grains of sand,
as much as the mountains and valleys and flat plains of land,
from the day You created the world until the day it ends,
every day a thousand times.

O Allah, we ask You to bless our Prophet Muhammad
as much as the grasses that dip and dance in the breeze,
as much as the leaves that spring and fall from the trees,
from the day You created the world until the day it ends,
every day a thousand times.

O Allah, we ask You to bless our Prophet Muhammad
as much as Your seven salt seas and all the creatures inside,
those that we know of and those that You hide,
from the day You created the world until the day it ends,
every day a thousand times.

O Allah, we ask You to bless our Prophet Muhammad
as much as the dewdrops that sparkle and the raindrops that pour,
as much as the rivers flow and waves lap the shore,
from the day You created the world until the day it ends,
every day a thousand times.

O Allah, we ask You to bless our Prophet Muhammad
as much as there are angels, people, and jinn,
as much as the hair on their bodies or the beat of their wings,
from the day You created the world until the day it ends,
every day a thousand times.

O Allah, we ask You to bless our Prophet Muhammad
as much as the crowing of roosters and the cooing of doves,
as much as the grazing of cattle and the crawling of bugs,
from the day You created the world until the Day it ends,
every day a thousand times

O Allah, we ask You to bless our Prophet Muhammad
as much as the winds that blow and the shadows that creep,
as much as the winding of turbans and the dreams of those asleep,
from the day You created the world until the day it ends,
every day a thousand times.

O Allah, we ask You to bless our Prophet Muhammad
as much as is pleasing to You,
as much as is pleasing to him and makes You pleased with us too,
from the day You created the world until the day of Qiyama,
every day a thousand times.

O Allah bless Muhammad, the most and the best
Of all the creation that You've ever blessed.
Keep our eyes fixed on the way that he showed,
Our feet firmly planted on his plainly marked road.
Make us kindly and caring, helpful and humble
So we don't fall by the wayside or linger or stumble.

Keep our tongue moist with the Noble Quran,
Our heart in dhikr, and our hand in his hand.
May we rest in his shade and drink from his well.
May we ride our buraq safely over the fires of hell.
May we act with wisdom and behave in good manner
And stand shoulder to shoulder in ranks under his banner.
May our light shine before us and from our right hand.
With the pure and the truthful may we take our stand.

May our love for him grow until it reaches farther
Than our love for our mother or love for our father.
For however much we love him, he loves us more.
He will wait till the last one of us reaches the shore
Of Your Mercy Oceans and Your Paradise Door.

O Allah please bless all the Muslims who were good or who tried,
The ones still living and the ones who have died.
Bless the rich and the poor, the happy and the sad.
Please bless all the believers, the good and even the bad.

We ask for Your blessings on our master Muhammad,

The one You have chosen to be Your Beloved.

O Allah bless him a thousand times more than the rest

Of Your vast creation that You have so abundantly blessed.

Bless him as he deserves, and only You know that best.

O Allah bless our master Muhammad,
whose heart was so full of Your Majesty,
whose eyes were so full of Your Beauty,
whose words were so full of Your Truth,
whose hands were so full of Your Justice,
whose smile was so full of Your Love
that he never lost hope,
he never felt alone,
and he never failed.
O Allah please bless Your Prophet Muhammad
And all of his family and companions.

Addendum

Allah says about Himself in Quran that He counts all things big and small:

He takes count, one by one, of everything [that exists] (72:28)
Verily God keeps count of all things (4:86)

Counting is a very human thing to do, certainly a very Muslim thing to do, as we were made to resemble our Maker even in the small things. He asks us to keep count of the cycles of prayer, of the praises we say, of the days of the month, of the months of the year. We count our harvest, our wealth, our inheritance, to make sure we give everyone their rightful share. It was just this interest in counting that inspired Muslim mathematicians to develop algebra and expand on the use of the zero. Without the zero how would we ever be able to write such enormous numbers or figure out the numbers of things we cannot see and can hardly imagine?

When we ask Allah to bless the Prophet (sas) as many times as there are stars in the sky or water in the sea, just what is it we are asking? The following pages are just for fun, for those of you who like to count or are interested in unusual facts.

Number Chart – Count the zeros

100 – 1 hundred -379 feet is the tallest tree in the world, a redwood in California.

1,000 - 1 thousand – 1,440 minutes in a day.

10,000 –10 thousand – circumference of the earth is 24,901 miles.

100,000 – 100 thousand – 238,900 miles from the earth to the moon.

1,000,000 – 1 million – 2,678,400 seconds in a month

10,000,000 – 10 million – 92,960,000 miles is the distance from the earth to the sun

100,000,000 – 100 million – the number of words you speak in a lifetime, 860,000,000.

1,000,000,000 - 1 billion – 1.6 billion Muslims in the world.

1,000,000,000,000 – 1 trillion – there are around 3.5 trillion fish in the sea.

1,000,000,000,000,000 - 1 quadrillion – the number of ants in the world is a 100 quadrillion

1,000,000,000,000,000,000 – 1 quintillion – is the number of mm to the closest star.

1,000,000,000,000,000,000,000 - 1 sextillion – 500 sextillion is the number of stars in the universe.

1,000,000,000,000,000,000,000,000 – 1 septillion – the weight of the earth is 6 septillion kg.

1,000,000,000,000,000,000,000,000,000 – 1 octillion – the number of peas to fill a hollow earth.

O Allah, we ask You to bless our Prophet Muhammad

as much as the day takes turns with the night,

as much as the darkness hides and the dawn brings to light,

from the day You created the world until the day it ends,

every day a thousand times.

Days and Nights

We don't know when Allah created the world. Geologists say the earth is four and a half billion years old (4,500,000,000) and astronomers say the universe is around fourteen billion years old (14,000,000,000). Allah hasn't told us in The Quran, although He did say that He created the heavens and earth in 6 days. We don't know how long those days were because in one place in The Quran He says that some of His days are equal to 1,000 (one thousand) of our years (22:47) and in another place He says that some of His days are equal to 50,000 (fifty thousand) of our years (70:4). Allah's time is His own, He is beyond time.

And we certainly don't know when He will bring our world to an end, although astronomers predict that will happen five billion years (5,000,000,000) from now when our sun burns up all its fuel, while environmentalists say it could happen much sooner because of global warming. But it is Allah who knows these things best and He has only told us that what has a beginning must also have an end. Only He is without beginning or end and He is now as He always was.

For our purpose we can just count from the day they say the Prophet Muhammad (sas) was born. There have been about 1,446 (one thousand, four hundred and forty six) years, which is 528,151 (five hundred and twenty eight thousand, one hundred and fifty one) days since April 20th 570, which is the day some people figure was the Prophet's (sas) birthday, until April 20th 2016. Can you figure out how many years and days since you were born?

The night and day take turns twice on each and every day with a sunrise and a sunset. So we have to double the last figure. That results in 1,060,000 (1 million, 60 thousand) times. Then we are asking to multiply that by another 1,000.

That means we are asking Allah to bless our Prophet with at least 1,060,000,000 (one billion, sixty million) praises in every day. If we said one praising on the Prophet every second, it would take us about 33 years to do this ourselves - that is if we praised straight, without stopping to eat or sleep or anything else.

Fortunately we can say things with our heart much faster than with our tongue, so maybe with Allah's help we could do it in a bit less time than this. And since for every good deed we do, Allah has promised to reward us with 10, the time could be reduced to just 3 years, 4 months. But asking Allah to do it for us is a much wiser course. And it is the course that the Prophet (sas) himself recommended when he gave advice to a lady who was using date pits to count out thousands of praises of Allah. He told her it would be better for her to simply ask that Allah be praised as much as all He created in the heavens, as much as all He created on the earth, and as much as everything in between. (at-Tirmidhi)

'Subhan-Allahi 'adada ma khalaqa fis-sama', wa subhan-Allahi 'adada ma khalaqa fil-ardi, wa subhan-Allahi 'adada ma baina dhalika,

Allah's counting is different than ours. If His day is equal to 1,000 of our years then it would only take Him 2 hours 30 minutes to praise His Prophet (sas) as much as we are asking. And of course, His blessing is of much greater benefit than ours because He knows the true value of all things and what He wills is what happens, and that is exactly what our noble Prophet (sas) deserves.

O Allah, we ask You to bless our Prophet Muhammad

as much as the circling of planets and the pulsing of stars,

as much as the glorifying of angels and the beating of hearts,

from the day You created the world until the day it ends,

every day a thousand times.

Stars

If you look up at the sky on a clear moonless night, in a place without electric lights, from any spot on the earth you should be able to see about 2,500 (two thousand, five hundred) stars. If you live in a city with lots of electric lights, you will see many, many, fewer than that. So if that is the number of stars visible in the sky from the half of the world in darkness, then you have to double it for the other half, which is facing the sun. Because even if the sun is shining too brightly for us to see, the stars are still there twinkling. And from the North and South Poles you can always see about 5,000 stars every night of the year. Altogether the sky visible to the unaided eye contains roughly 5,000 (five thousand) stars.

With binoculars you can see up to 100,000 (one hundred thousand) stars. With a 3inch telescope you can see up to 1,000,000 (one million) stars. With an astronomer's telescope in a remote place you should be able to increase that number to about 200,000,000 (two hundred million) stars.

The most powerful Hubble telescope, in orbit, looking from the darkness of space, can catch the light of approximately 400 billion objects. 200 billion of these are stars in our galaxy. The other 200 billion are so far away that although they appear to be stars they are really whole galaxies. Each one of these 200 billion galaxies contains at least 200 billion stars of their own. Scientists now estimate that there are at least 500,000,000,000,000,000,000,000 (five hundred sextillion) stars in the universe – one of which is our sun. And they are still counting. And just to put that in perspective, it has been estimated that the human body contains seventy trillion cells. So there might be about as many cells inside all the people of the earth as there are stars in the sky.

Angels

We don't know the number of angels. We have been told that at all times 70,000 (seventy thousand) of them circle around the Baytu l-Ma'mur, the heavenly Ka'ba which sits directly above above the earthly Ka'ba. Every day they leave and a different 70,000 take their place. This has been going on since the world was made and no angel ever circles a second day. We don't know when the world was made but geologists say that the earth is 4,500,000,000 (four billion, five hundred million) years old. With 365 days in each year, that would make at least 115,000,000,000,000,000 (one hundred and fifteen quadrillion) angels who have circled the Baytu l-Ma'mur since the possible creation of the earth. And almost 37,000,000,000 (thirty seven billion) angels that have circled it since the day the Prophet was born.

We have been told that each of us has 2 angels with us at all times and that each living thing has its guardian angel as well. So this means that everything we are counting has its counterpart angel.

The earth is full of angels. The Prophet (sas) said that the heavens are groaning under the weight of the angels. There is not even an empty space the width of 4 fingers without an angel praying there. Since angels are made from light they do not take up as much space as we do.

The Quran says about angels that: *"They glorify Him tirelessly night and day." (21:20)*

The main job of all these uncountable angels is to glorify their Lord. This is what they were created to do and they never get bored and they never get tired.

Hearts

As for the human heart, using an average of 80 beats a minute, the average human heart beats 4,800 (four thousand, eight hundred) times an hour. That is 115, 200 (one hundred and fifteen thousand, two hundred) times in a day. If you live to be 80 years old, your heart will have beaten 3,363,840,000 (three billion, three hundred and sixty three million, eight hundred and forty thousand) times in your life. Can you feel your heart beating? Can you count the number of times it beats in a minute?

Now multiply that number of beats in a lifetime by the number of people who have ever lived, which they say is, 107,000,000,000 (one hundred and seven billion) and, well, you have an even bigger number, 359,930,880,000,000,000,000 (three hundred and fifty nine quintillion, nine hundred and thirty quadrillion, eight hundred and eighty trillion).

And that is just counting human hearts. Of course animals and birds, fish and insects, all have beating hearts as well. And each one of those hearts is beating to the same tune – Allah, Allah, Allah – whether we hear them or understand them, whether we stop to count them or not.

And as tiny as the human heart might be and as great and vast and unfathomable as Allah Almighty is – that valiant human heart is the only thing in the universe that has the possibility to hold its Lord. But then that is the spiritual heart, not the physical heart, and that leads us to a different level of meaning altogether.

O Allah, we ask You to bless our Prophet Muhammad

as much as the rocks and gravel and grains of sand,

as much as the mountains and valleys and flat plains of land

from the day You created the world until the day it ends,

every day a thousand times.

Sand

Someone counted the number of grains of sand in a teaspoon and then multiplied that number by the many acres of beaches and deserts that have been mapped by satellite, including how deep they are thought to be. They came up with a number for all the grains of sand in the whole world: 7,500,000,000,000,000,000,000 (seven sextillion, five hundred quintillion). And as big as that is, there are 67 times that number of stars in the universe.

And all those stars with all their grains of sand were made by Allah and are kept spinning and traveling on paths we cannot see, to destinations we cannot imagine, by His word.

Mountains

According to some, a mountain is a wrinkle or bump on the earth's surface that rises 2,000 feet (610 meters) or more. Anything smaller than that is called a hill. But not all people agree on this definition. In order to count something you have to know what it is and what it isn't. How high does a mountain have to be to be called a mountain? Often mountains come in ranges, which means that mountains are connected to each other, although their peaks are separate. If you can isolate a single mountain, do you measure its height up from the level of the ground, or from the level of the sea, or as some suggest, from the center of the earth?

Almost one quarter of the earth's surface is covered by mountains. There are 10,000 peaks above 1500 meters and 109 peaks above 7000 meters. There are volcanoes that rise from the floor of the ocean and tower above the level of the sea, making large islands like Hawaii for people to live on. There are thousands of mountains and volcanoes however, that never reach above the surface of the sea, underwater mountains that have never been climbed or counted.

Mountains, rising out of the plains, act as barriers to clouds. In order to pass over a mountain, a rain cloud has to drop some of its water. The cloud then becomes lighter and floats higher until it can pass over the mountain. As the rain runs down the side of the mountain and onto the plain, the moving water makes grooves or channels in the earth. These are called valleys, and they run as far and as long as needed to carry the rainwater downhill to the sea. It is a system Allah created to keep our precious water circulating between heaven and earth.

O Allah, we ask You to bless our Prophet Muhammad

as much as the grasses that dip and dance in the breeze,

as much as the leaves that spring and fall from the trees,

from the day You created the world until the day it ends,

every day a thousand times.

Blades of Grass

They estimate that an average of 10 grass plants grow in a 10 cm square. You could try this for yourself by laying your hand over a patch of grass and counting the plants. Lawn grass grows thickly but wild grass grows thin and tall. Most of the grass in the world is wild. There are one billion (1,000,000,000) blades of grass in a square kilometer.

Of the surface of the earth only 29% is dry land and out of that only 20% is grassland, plains, prairie, and meadow, while the rest is made up of deserts and beaches, mountains and forests, cities and parking lots. There are about sixteen million (16,000,000) square kilometers of grassland on earth.

If you multiply the number of blades of grass in a square kilometer by the number of square kilometers of grassland on earth, you get 16,000,000,000,000,000 (sixteen quadrillion) blades of grass over the entire surface of the earth. How many are in your yard or park?

Leaves

Try counting the leaves on a tree where you live. You will see there are many kinds of big and small trees and many kinds of leaves. Pines trees have leaves like green needles and they have thousands of them in bunches on their branches. Palm trees just have a few large leaves, or fronds, that grow out from the very top of the tree. So we take an average, which means, if you divided all the leaves evenly among all the trees it would be the number of leaves each tree would have. Experts say that there are about three trillion (3,000,000,000,000) living, breathing trees in the world. If this estimate is true, there are almost 420 (four hundred and twenty) trees for each person.

They say on average there are 100,000 (one hundred thousand) leaves on each tree. That gives us an approximate answer of 300,000,000,000,000,000 (three hundred quadrillion) leaves in the world at any one time. Of course this is only a rough estimate that does not even include leaves that grow on plants other than trees.

If you wanted to count each and every leaf yourself, and if you could move around fast enough to count a leaf a second, it would take you eight billion (8,000,000,000) years to just count all the leaves. That is almost twice the age of the planet itself. And as winter comes and old leaves start falling and then spring arrives and new leaves appear, you would have to start counting all over again before you had even hardly gotten started.

O Allah, we ask You to bless our Prophet Muhammad

as much as Your seven salt seas and all the creatures inside,

those that we know of and those that You hide,

from the day You created the world until the day it ends,

every day a thousand times.

Sea Creatures

There are scientists around the world counting the contents of the seas right now. But before you can count something you have to define what it is, so that you know what is a part of it and what is a part of something else. As of today there are 228,450 (two hundred twenty eight thousand, four hundred and fifty) different species of marine life, from seaweed to whale. But they think there must be at least 1 or 2 million more to be discovered. In fact scientists estimate that almost 91% of marine species are yet to be discovered. And a species is just a category of creature that can be scientifically defined and distinguished from other kinds. It is a group of individuals. Scientists are not even ready to guess how many individuals there are within each species.

Whales are the largest creatures in the sea. They need the most room to live and the most food to eat and are the most visible so they should be easiest to count. There should be fewer of them than of the smaller creatures like sardines, or jellyfish, or the tiny krill that some whales eat. There are thought to be two million (2,000,000) whales. A hundred years ago there were as many as three million but because of reckless hunting practices their numbers have been drastically reduced. It is estimated that there are 3,500,000,000,000 (three and a half trillion) fish swimming in oceans of the world. This amounts to 467 fish for each person.

Living in the salty water of the sea, there are many, many creatures we know of and then there are even more creatures still hidden from us, waiting to be found. So asking Allah to praise the Prophet (sas) as many times as the creatures in the sea is a task, that for the moment, only Allah is able to do. We have not even come close.

O Allah, we ask You to bless our Prophet Muhammad

as much as the dewdrops sparkle and the raindrops pour,

as much as the rivers flow and waves lap the shore,

from the day You created the world until the day it ends,

every day a thousand times.

Drops of Water

Some experts have measured how much rain falls into their rain-collecting gauge in an average storm – how many inches or centimeters of water were collected in that tube during the storm. Then they find out from satellite pictures how big an area the storm covered.

Then they measure the size of a single raindrop. This can be more complicated than you would think. Apparently there are different size raindrops. They think that most drops leave their cloud at about the same size but on their way down they burst into drops of differing sizes. The English and the American scientists calculate different sizes for the average drop. If all the rain in an average storm cloud joined together into one huge drop, that drop would be over 1 kilometer across and would weigh six million tons (6,000,000). It would crash onto the earth and flood and destroy everything for 20-30 kilometers around. So we can thank God that rain falls in drops!

Then imagine that if the whole area of the storm were a big bucket as deep as the amount of rain that collected in the tube, how many tiny raindrops would fit in that bucket. They came up with a very big number: one trillion, six hundred and twenty billion (1,620,000,000,000) raindrops fall in a single average storm. And in a year they estimate that around seven quintillion (7,000,000,000,000,000,000) raindrops fall to earth.

That is more than there are trees to catch them and approximately 23 raindrops for every leaf on earth. A trillion of anything is so big that if you had a trillion dollars and you spent 1 million dollars every day, it would take you 2,739 (two thousand, seven hundred and thirty nine) years to finish all your money and a quintillion is a million times more than that. If you spread a quintillion pennies out like a carpet, one next to the other, they would be able to blanket the whole planet earth twice.

Scientists say that the oceans cover 70% of the earth's surface. They estimate that all the oceans on earth contain about three hundred and fifty two quintillion (352,000,000,000,000,000,000) gallons of water. And each gallon of water contains about 100,000 (one hundred thousand) drops. They say there are altogether 20,000,000,000,000,000,000,000,000 (twenty septillion) drops in the ocean.

You could actually count the number of drops in a cup if you have a leaky faucet, a measuring cup, and the patience to sit counting to 6,250 (six thousand, two hundred and fifty). A gallon contains 16 cups. If you could drink a gallon of water every hour, it would take you 352,000,000,000,000,000,000 (three hundred and fifty two quintillion) hours or 40,182,648,401,826,488 (around forty quadrillion) years to drink up all the oceans. Well that is just silly because, if you were by some chance to live that long, why would you want to spend your whole life drinking briny sea water?

But the most amazing thing is that scientists know that inside just 1,000 tiny drops of water are as many molecules as there are drops of water in all the vast oceans of the earth.

O Allah, we ask You to bless our Prophet Muhammad

as much as there are angels, people, and jinn,

as much as the hair on their bodies or the beat of their wings,

from the day You created the world until the day it ends,

every day a thousand times.

Numbers of People

We don't know about angels and jinn, what they look like or how many there are. They are part of the unseen, those things that Allah and His Prophet (sas) have told us about but which we can't see. We must believe in their existence and their influence on us, even if we can't see them with our eyes, because Allah and His Prophet (sas) have told us about them. We believe without seeing. We take it on faith. We also must take it on faith that some scientist has counted all the molecules in a drop of water or that molecules even exist.

The number of people alive on the planet has, however, been counted. Most countries take a census every 10 years or so to see how many people they have, usually so they can tax them. There is a site on the Internet that shows the population of the earth and how it changes every second with predicted births and deaths. At the time this was written, Friday the 5th of August 2016 at 10:30pm, it said there were 7,441,321,400 (seven billion four hundred and forty one million, three hundred and twenty one thousand, four hundred) people alive on the earth.

Have you ever tried to count the number of people in your family, your aunts and uncles, cousins and their cousins? An average soccer stadium holds 70,000 (seventy thousand) people. You would need at least 106,305 (one hundred and six thousand, three hundred and five) stadiums to hold all the people of the earth.

They estimate that the number of people, who have ever lived – all those alive today plus all those who have already died - is one hundred and seven billion (107,000,000,000). We know that every person has at least 2 angels that stay with them their whole lives, one on the right shoulder, who writes all their good deeds in a book, and one on the left shoulder, who writes all their bad deeds in another book. The Prophet (sas) has told us that each of us also has a tempting devil jinn that accompanies us throughout our lives, whispering in our ears to do things that are not right. So that means there are at least seven billion devils on duty in the world today, which is a terrible thought except that there are also at least double that number of angels, al-hamdu liLlah!

Hair

So the next question is, how many hairs do those people have on their heads and bodies?

Human beings have an average of 100,000 (one hundred thousand) hairs on their heads. They have, however, four million nine hundred thousand (4,900,000) hairs on the rest of their body. Which is just about as much hair as a primate has on its body, only our hairs are finer and thinner and not so visible. Altogether each person has around five million (5,000,000) hairs.

So then if there are one hundred and seven billion (107,000,000,000) people who have ever lived and each one of them had five million hairs, that would add up to five hundred and thirty five sextillion (535,000,000,000,000,000,000) hairs to make blessing on the Prophet (sas). And that of course doesn't take into account the hairs of devils and jinn who, I have been told, are a good deal hairier than we are. But angels, who are made of light, probably have little to no hair although when they assume a human form they would then appear to have hair like a human.

Wings

Human beings don't have wings but it is said that one kind of jinn do. There is a hadith of the Prophet (sas) saying that there are three kinds of Jinn. One kind can take the shape of animals or birds, one kind moves like the wind, rests and then moves on again, and one kind has wings

We know that angels have wings. Quran says that they have 2, 3 or 4 (35:1). The Prophet Muhammad (sas) told us after his Mi'raj to the Heavens, that he saw angels with thousands of wings. Jibrail (as) is described as having 600 (six hundred) mighty wings which, when spread, covered the whole sky. One enormous angel named Hizqil has altogether 18,000 (eighteen thousand) wings.

So what kind of numbers are we talking about when we ask for as many blessings on the Prophet (sas) as the beat of their wings?

Let's talk about bird wings since we don't know anything about devil or jinn wings. It depends on the size and weight of the bird and the nature of its flight. A hummingbird flaps 80 times in a second to hover the way it does. A big vulture flaps his wings only 1 time in a second, once he is in flight. A blue jay is somewhere in between them at 40 flaps a second. An eagle flaps his wings 5 times a second.

So a hummingbird flaps 4,800 (four thousand eight hundred) times a minute, 288,000 (two hundred and eighty eight thousand) times an hour. And a blue jay 2,400 (two thousand, four hundred) times a minute and 144,000 (one hundred and forty four thousand) times an hour.

Even if jinn and devils are heavy creatures, more like eagles or pterodactyls than like humming birds, that still amounts to 60 flaps a minute. Geologists date the earth to be 4,500,000,000 (four billion, five hundred million) years old. That means it is approximately 142,000,000,000,000,000 (one hundred and forty two quadrillion) seconds old and, if they flap their wings once a second, that is also the number of flaps of one of their kind since the creation of the planet. Multiply that by the number of jinn and devils, which is probably about the same as the number of people, and you get the number we are asking Allah Almighty to send praises on the Prophet (sas).

We cannot even begin to estimate the number of angels or the number of their wings. Anyway you look, imagine, or count - that is a lot of beating, flapping, and a lot of praising.

O Allah, we ask You to bless our Prophet Muhammad

as much as the crowing of roosters and the cooing of doves,

as much as the grazing of cattle and the crawling of bugs,

from the day You created the world until the Day it ends,

every day a thousand times.

Roosters, Doves, Cows, and Bugs

The United Nations figures that there is an average of over twenty billion (20,000,000,000,000) chickens alive on earth at any time. Of these perhaps only one billion are roosters because if there are too many roosters they fight each other to the death. The roosters protect the hens and ward off danger. One way they do this is by crowing loudly to scare off predators or to warn the flock. According to our Prophet (sas) however, the roosters perform another important function. They tell us when it is time to pray. They begin to crow as much as 2 hours before sunrise to help us get up for night praying and for Fajr.

There is an angel who sits on Allah's throne, who has the shape of a very large white rooster. He crows the adhan to inform the angelic hosts to gather for prayer. Some of the earthly roosters hear his call and they also begin to crow to alert the earthly believers that the time for prayer has arrived. They crow before dawn and then every 5 minutes or so until the sun has risen. They also crow periodically during the day. So if we estimate on the low side that they crow 5 times a day for the 5 prayers and every 5 minutes between Fajr and Shuruq, that would be a minimum of 30 crows a day. For all of the one billion (1,000,000,000) roosters on earth that would amount to at least thirty billion crows a day (30,000,000,000). Anyone living near a rooster can confirm that they usually crow more than 30 times in a day.

The Museum of Natural History says there are between 200 and 400 billion (200,000,000,000 or 400,000,000,000) individual birds flying around this planet, which is a wide guess, either 200 billion or double that. But at the lowest number that would make about 29 birds for each person.

Pigeons and doves are the most common birds in the world. It is estimated that there are

400,000,000 (four hundred million) doves and pigeons, of which 1,000,000 (one million) live in New York City alone. And, as any New Yorker can probably tell you, pigeons coo constantly, maybe even in their sleep.

Even though the earth is 91% water, almost 86% of the animals and plants live on dry land and most of these are bugs. It is estimated that at any one time there are ten quintillion (10,000,000,000,000,000,000) insects alive on the earth. That means there are 1.5 million bugs for each and every person. I hope mine are not the kind that bite!

There are around 100,000,000,000,000,000 (one hundred quadrillion) ants in the world, about 6 ants for every blade of grass. Some termite ant colonies in South Africa have over 3,000,000 (three million) occupants, which is about the same as the population of Rome.

They estimate that there are 10 wild animals (mostly rabbits, squirrels, and mice) for every human being on the earth. That would make around 74,000,000,000 (seventy four billion) wild animals living beside us. And there are an estimated 1,500,000,000 (one billion, five hundred million) cows munching grass or chewing their cud around the world at any given moment.

O Allah, we ask You to bless our Prophet Muhammad

as much as the winds that blow and the shadows that creep,

as much as the winding of turbans and the dreams of those asleep,

from the day You created the world until the day of Qiyama,

every day a thousand times.

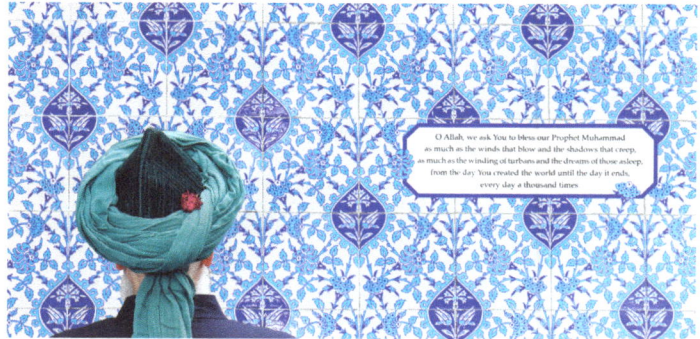

Dreams

At any one time maybe one third of all the people are sleeping so that is 2,480,440,467 (two billion, four hundred and eighty million, four hundred and forty thousand, four hundred and sixty seven) sleeping people. But since all people have to sleep at some time, we can count all the people 7,441,321,400 (seven billion, four hundred and forty one million, three hundred and twenty one thousand, four hundred). And researchers say that everyone dreams 4 or 6 dreams a night whether they remember them or not. If we multiply the number of people by an average of 5 dreams a night we get 37,206,607,000 (thirty seven billion, two hundred and six million, six hundred and seven thousand) dreams every 24 hours happening around the world.

Looking at it in another way, a person dreams 5 times a night for 365 nights of the year. She dreams 1,825 dreams every year. If she lives for 50 years she will have dreamed an average of 91,250 in her lifetime. Multiply that number by the number of people who have ever lived and slept on this planet and you get 9,763,750,000,000,000 (nine quadrillion, seven hundred and sixty three trillion, seven hundred and fifty billion) dreams dreamed on this beautiful blue planet since people began dreaming.

And that doesn't take into account all the animals who, scientists say, also dream.

Turbans

As for the winding of turbans, that is a very small number in comparison to the enormous numbers we have been talking about. But some things are important even if they are small. A small turban may be just 3 turns or circles of cloth. A large turban can be 30 turns.

The Prophet (sas) wore a turban and there are many Hadith in which he is said to have advised his followers to wear one also. He called it the crown of the Arabs and said it is what the angels wear. Its winding will increase patience in the wearer and it distinguishes the Muslim from the non-believer. He said that wearing a turban for prayer brings more reward.

His companions have told us that the Prophet (sas) had both long turban cloths and short ones, white, black, red, and green. The one in the Topkapi Museum is green. He wound it leaving a tail that hung down his back between his shoulder blades. This is what we call his sunnah, his way.

O Allah, we ask You to bless our Prophet Muhammad

as much as is pleasing to You,

as much as is pleasing to him and makes You pleased with us too,

from the day You created the world until the day of Qiyama,

every day a thousand times.

We should live our lives always keeping in mind what it is that will make Allah pleased with us. To believe in Him, His Angels, His Books, His Prophets, the Day of Judgment, and Destiny – that both the good and the bad are from Him; to keep our prayers, to give charity, to fast Ramadan, to make the pilgrimage to Mecca if we are able; to remember Allah in all we do, to obey His Prophet and to ask for blessings on him and his family, to treat those around us as we want to be treated ourselves - these are the things that make Allah pleased with us.

And yet with all of this I think Allah is easier to please than we are. So remember it is also our job to be pleased with our Lord, who has given us everything we have - our eyes to see, our ears to hear, our mouths to count, our brains to figure, and our hearts to be grateful and loving. And if there is one thing in the universe that is impossible to try to count, it would be our Lord's gifts.

He gives you all that you ask of Him and should you try to count Allah's blessings, you can never compute them. (14:34)

And as gigantic and mind boggling as all these enormous numbers of big things are, there are even larger numbers of small things. So that the number of molecules in ten tiny drops of water is the same as the number of all the stars in the universe that we can see.

And if you think that these big numbers are amazing, then think of all the wonderful fantastic things that they are counting, in all their variety and color and form and uniqueness. Then try to think how more amazing and great is the One, who created them all. Allah is more amazing and bigger and greater and beyond all our attempts to count or imagine. No matter how awesome all these huge numbers may be, the most awesome number is really the first. 1 is where all counting begins and Allah is 1.

And to take the point philosophically farther: if we can be 0 – meaning if we can be in complete obedience and compliance with Allah, with no opposition to what He wants - in the language of the Sufis, if we can be nothing - then our nothingness added to Allah's unity becomes something of immense value.

The Prophet gave us all of his love and all of his care and spent his life trying to show us the best way to live and the smooth path to follow for everlasting happiness. We owe him our love and gratitude. We owe him everything. And we wish for him the best of everything Allah has to give. And we try to understand the hadith that says, if we don't love him more than we love our mother and our father, more than we love even our own selves, then our understanding is weak and our faith is incomplete.

In conclusion we send our greetings and praise to the Beloved, Sayyiduna Muhammad (sas), and we ask Allah to do the counting for us, not only because His counting is infinite and everlasting, but mostly because His love is infinite and everlasting and that is what our most kind and noble Prophet (sas) deserves.

Verily Allah and His Angels bless the Prophet. O you who believe, ask blessings on him and greet him with a greeting of peace. (33:56)

Allahuma salli wa sallam wa barak ala Sayyidana Muhammad wa ala alihi was sahbihi ajama'in.

Photo Credits

www.ingramcontent.com/pod-product-compliance
Lightning Source LLC
Chambersburg PA
CBHW060812090426

42737CB00002B/45